How to Babysit an
Orangutan

Story and Photographs by
Tara Darling and Kathy Darling

Walker and Company
New York

First published in the United States of America in 1996 by Walker Publishing Company, Inc.

Published simultaneously in Canada by Thomas Allen & Son Canada, Limited, Markham, Ontario

Library of Congress Cataloging-in-Publication Data
Darling, Kathy
How to babysit an orangutan/Kathy Darling; photographs by Tara Darling
p. cm.
Includes index.
Summary: Describes how baby orangutans whose mothers have died are nurtured by human babysitters at Camp Leakey in the rain forests of Borneo, until they are ready to live in the wild.
ISBN 0-8027-8466-6 (hardcover). —ISBN 0-8027-8467-4 (reinforced binding)
1. Orangutan—Infancy—Juvenile literature. 2. Wildlife reintroduction—Juvenile literature. [1. Orangutan. 2. Animals—Infancy. 3. Wildlife reintroduction. 4. Wildlife conservation.]
I. Darling, Tara, ill. II. Title.
QL737.P96D354 1996
599.88'42—dc20
96-5445
CIP
AC

Map on page 33 by Susan and Mark Carlson

Book design by Marva J. Martin

Printed in Hong Kong

2 4 6 8 10 9 7 5 3 1

THE ORANGUTAN FOUNDATION INTERNATIONAL
Research - Conservation - Education

Dear Reader,

In this book you will read about an orangutan named Princess. When she was five years old, I was her babysitter. At Camp Leakey I helped my foster child learn how to survive in the rain forest of Borneo. So that I could teach her things, I taught her sign language—the same sign language that deaf people use.

Princess is one of our success stories. She is a wild orangutan again. But she has not forgotten her friends at Camp Leakey and comes to visit us often. Even as adults, orangutans need help, though. So in 1986 Dr. Galdikas, myself, and several other people started the Orangutan Foundation International as a way to help Princess and the other orangutans.

If you read How to Babysit an Orangutan you will learn about that work. Then you can get involved too. On the jacket of the book is the information about how you can become a foster parent.

Regards,

Gary Shapiro, Ph.D.

822 S. Wellesley Ave., Los Angeles, California 90049
(310) 207-1655; FAX: (310) 207-1556

How do you babysit an orangutan?
Well, first you have to find an
orangutan that needs babysitting.
    That's easy here at Camp Leakey.
Located in the middle of a rain
forest on the island of Borneo,
Camp Leakey is not your average
camp. It's really an orangutan
orphanage.

Nanang, my favorite orangutan.

Orangutans at Camp Leakey like to hug.

Ordinarily, orangutan babies don't need human babysitters, but the mothers of these little red apes have been killed and the orphans are too young to survive alone in the jungle. Without babysitters, all the babies would die from disease, starvation, or injuries.

On the way to the forest to play.

My friend Birute Galdikas is teaching me how to be an orangutan sitter. For more than twenty years she has been taking care of orangutan babies and training babysitters at Camp Leakey.

The first thing she told me was that babysitting an orangutan is not a "forever" job. A good babysitter's job is done when the baby grows up and can go off into the rain forest and live as a wild ape.

Our job is to teach the orphans the skills they need to get along on their own. That usually takes until they are seven or eight years old, the age when they would leave their natural mother. Then we must say good-bye.

Study time in the rain forest.

This is not easy. Orangutan babies are cute and cuddly and especially loving. These are the qualities that landed them in the orphanage in the first place. A lot of people think the adorable apes would be good pets, so greedy animal dealers can get a lot of money for one of the endangered babies. But mother orangutans will not give up their babies without a fight and they are usually killed by the baby snatchers. Then the little orphans are smuggled out of Borneo and Sumatra, the only place the remaining 5,000 wild orangs live. For every baby that reaches a circus, private zoo, or movie trainer, eight orangutans don't survive the trip.

Only a few of the babies are lucky enough to be rescued and brought back to the rain forest. They need tropical forests to find food, and the forests are disappearing as fast as the orangutans, which once numbered in the millions.

Orangutans are very good mothers.

Milk is good for orangutan babies . . . in a bottle

Five-year-old Nanang is my special favorite, but I am also helping with other orphans. Those under two years old take a lot of time, so all the babysitters help with them. The infants are pretty helpless for the first couple of years, much like human children.

. . . in a cup

Wild orangutan mothers nurse their babies for five or six years. So, if babies under this age come to camp, we must give them milk. Twice a day we mix up a big bucket of powdered cow's milk. Infants get the milk in a bottle. Three- and four-year-olds prefer to drink from a cup, and the wise-guy five- and six-year-olds think it is cool to slurp right from the bucket.

. . . or in a bucket!

Bananas are the babies' favorite food.

The babies depend on us for all their food. Like most children, baby orangutans are messy eaters. Babysitters must be prepared to have some food spit at them. Although we feed the babies a lot of bananas, we try to get our charges to eat foods that wild orangutans eat. Fruit is the main part of an orangutan's diet, but they also dine on nuts, flowers, leaves, and many plants that grow in the jungle. The only animals they eat regularly are termites and ants.

Nanang knows that termites are tasty. He checks out all rotten wood and peers into holes in the ground to find delicious (to him) bugs.

I want little Nanang to grow up strong. I'm willing to take a sip of milk to show him that milk tastes good. I enjoy eating bananas with him. I'll even nibble on some leaves once in a while to encourage him to try them. But I absolutely, positively refuse to eat either termites or ants. Surely, insect eating goes beyond a babysitter's duty!

In the rain forest it rains a lot. (I am sure this does not come as much of a surprise to you.) To make sure a downpour doesn't take me by surprise, I wear a rain hat. Nanang is very jealous. He snatches my hat and plops it onto his own head whenever he can. He loves wearing it even though it is so big he can't see anything with it on.

Nanang the hat thief.

This baby is jealous that Nanang has my hat and has made himself a hat out of a leaf.

Nanang thinks I am trying to drown him when I give him a bath.

In a heavy rain, wild orangutans often hold leaf umbrellas over their heads. Orangutans don't like to get wet. That's why bath time is not fun for a babysitter. The littlest orangs get skin diseases and lose their hair in the hot months. It is the babysitter's unlucky chore to give medicine baths. There is a lot of screaming and biting during the bath.

Tom is almost grown and lives in the jungle most of the time.
On laundry day he comes to Camp Leakey to beg for some soap to eat.

Orangutans don't like baths, but they do love soap. When I do my wash, Tom always begs for a bar. He has rather unusual ideas about what to do with soap. He thinks of it as food, soaping his arm and sucking the lather off with great slurps of delight. I guess he never heard that washing your mouth out with soap was supposed to be a punishment.

After a shampoo, orangutans head up into the trees as fast as they can.

This adult male is so big that he has a hard time climbing in the trees.
The babysitters think he weighs more than three hundred pounds.

It isn't necessary to comb an orangutan's hair after a bath. No matter what you do, it will stick up in spiky red clumps. All the babies have this wild hairdo. As they get older, it will become more manageable. When the head hair lies flat, it is a sign that your baby is growing up. Another sign that an orangutan is almost ready to go off on its own is when the skin around the mouth and eyes turns from the pink baby color to the adult black.

When Nanang and I walk in the forest, we often meet Princess and her baby, Peter. Peter is the same age as Nanang and loves to play with him.

Peter taught me an ape-sitting lesson I never forgot: Save all snacks till you are off duty. One morning Peter snuggled up close, stuck his dirty finger into my mouth, and scooped out my bubble gum. Chuckling happily, he popped it into his own mouth.

Princess cuddles with her son, Peter.

Peter is watching what Princess is eating. They are hot peppers. He took one out of her mouth, ate it, and got terrible blisters on his lips!

Tara is showing Nanang which leaves are good to eat.

Orangutans, big and little, are food thieves! Most humans, including me, think this is disgusting. However, it's normal, healthy behavior for a young orangutan to share food with an adult. There are hundreds of different fruits and leaves in the rain forest. Some of them are delicious, but a few are deadly poison. A baby orangutan must learn to tell them apart. So mothers allow food snatching. That way young ones can recognize the smell and taste of safe foods.

Wrestling is great fun for baby orangutans. They tickle each other sometimes when they tumble around.

Tara doesn't like to play games with biting—but Nanang does!

If you babysit children, you will probably see temper tantrums. Well, orangutan babies have tantrums that are much the same. There is a lot of kicking and screaming. There is also biting! Lots of biting.

Orangutan games almost always include biting. Not only do the apes nip each other as they play, but they will bite the babysitter if they can.

This grown-up orangutan isn't smiling—she's trying to scare us with an angry face. And it's working.

Nanang is making angry kissing noises to show he doesn't want to come to bed.

A playful orangutan shows its bottom teeth. It looks like an angry face, but it isn't. Angry orangutans stick out their lips and make kissing noises to show their displeasure. They burp a lot too. A babysitter has to be able to read the facial expressions of the orangutans. If you mistake the really angry face, with both sets of teeth showing, for a grin, you will surely feel those teeth.

Orangutan babies hanging around. They are not always careful climbers and sometimes they fall. Most of the time they don't get hurt.

Best friends.

Most of the time, little orangutans have a happy face. They are very playful. "Best friends" form play groups with three or four members. Sometimes we are assigned to watch one baby and other times we get a whole play group.

Best friends do everything together. The little orphans are lonesome, and it seems almost like they adopt each other and form a family. They hang around together every day. Hanging around means something different to an orangutan. Any game that is fun on the ground is more fun when hanging in the trees.

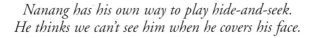

Nanang has his own way to play hide-and-seek.
He thinks we can't see him when he covers his face.

Tara is teaching Nanang to feel at home in the trees.

One of the most important lessons we teach to the orphan orangutans is that they belong in the trees. Every day we go to the forest so they can build muscles, practice balancing, and get the judgment and coordination necessary for life in the rain forest canopy. Thank goodness the babysitter is not required to climb into the trees with her charges. I couldn't begin to go where Nanang goes with ease. He can hang on with his feet as well as his hands. His wrists allow him to swivel around without changing grip. Even so, he falls once in a while. It takes a few years to get the hang of hanging around.

Nanang knows I can't climb very well. When it is bedtime, he climbs right to the very top of a tree. He hangs up there sucking his thumb till I lure him down with a banana snack.

Orangutan babies suck their thumbs just like human children do.

Princess is building a nest so she can take a nap. Peter is in it with her.

Nanang isn't old enough to sleep alone in the forest. A wild orangutan would sleep in its mother's nest for five or six years. Peter, for instance, still sleeps with Princess. There are some big snakes that could kill a sleeping baby.

Orangutans like a nice, soft place to sleep. Every night they make a new nest from leaves and branches. It takes about five or ten minutes to build one. The other great apes—gorillas and chimpanzees—also build tree nests, but only the orangutans put a roof on the top to keep out the rain. We can't show our charges how to build a nest in the trees. The best we can do is let them practice on the ground. The babies try to build a nest out of any materials they can find.

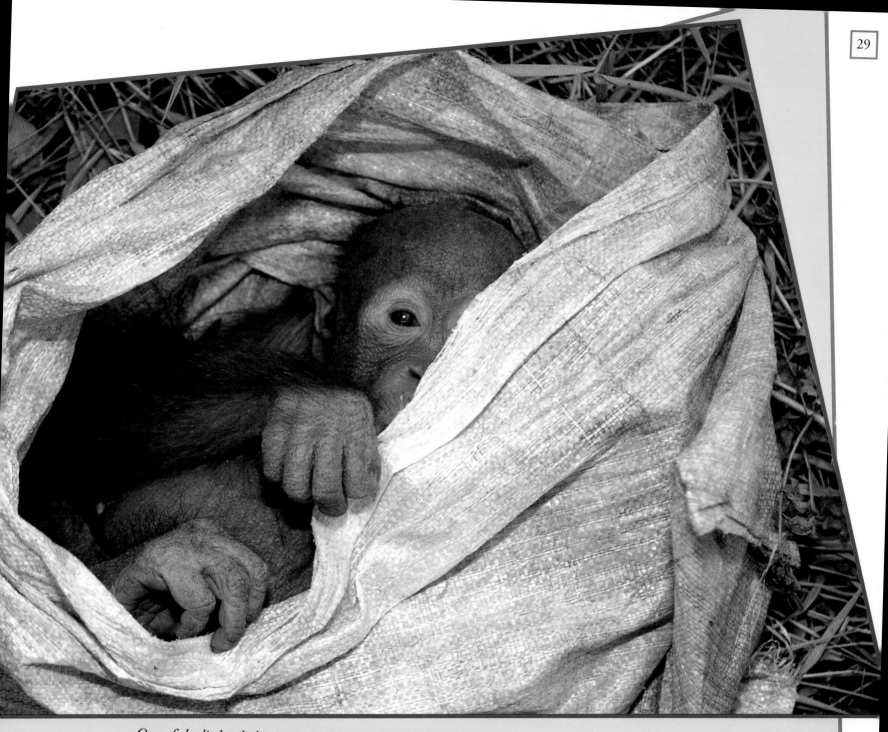

One of the littlest babies pretends an old sack is a nest. He brings bits of leaves and branches inside with him. Sack nests are great fun to play in.

Nanang is watching one of the older orangutans look for termites. The baby is too young to eat anything but milk yet.

Nest building is much easier to learn if the babies have an older ape to watch. When Camp Leakey was first built, there were only human babysitters. The little orangutans they raised grew up and went out into the forest. But not for good. Many live nearby and come often to visit. Some come with babies of their own. They are wonderful role models. Adult orangutans can teach the orphans things that human babysitters can't.

Every evening when I see Princess and Peter go walking off into the forest, it makes me happy. They are free. Free to climb in the canopy and free to come and visit when they want to.

Peter and Princess head back to the forest.

The babysitters at Camp Leakey have happily said good-bye to more than 100 orphans. These ex-captives have become wild again.

Although I love him very much, I hope someday I will be able to say good-bye to Nanang too.

ORANGUTAN FACTS

- **Asian ape.**
The orangutan is one of the three "great apes." The others are the gorilla and the chimpanzee of Africa.

- **Rain forest animal.**
Great apes are found only in tropical rain forests. Orangutans live on the islands of Borneo and Sumatra.

- **No tail.**
A quick way to tell apes from monkeys is to look for a tail. Most monkeys have tails but none of the apes do.

- **Males and females very different in size.**
Male orangutans are two or three times bigger than the 100-pound females.

- **Nine months pregnant.**
When they are ten years old, female orangutans can have babies. They average only three or four babies in their 35-year lifetime.

- **Babies stay with mother for six or seven years.**
Father never babysits.

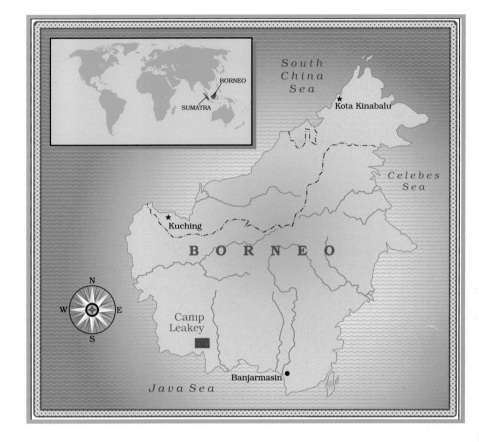

- **Single-mother families.**
All adult male orangutans live alone in the treetops.

- **Treetop singers.**
Orangutans rarely come to the ground. Males call out in search of mates in a loud voice that can be heard for miles.

INDEX